PROPERTY OF
WILL ROGERS SCHOOLS
3909 E. 5TH PLACE
TULSA, OKLAHOMA 74112

@2019 PROJECT EÑYE ALL RIGHTS RESERVED

All rights reseved. No part of this publication may be reproduced or transmitted in any form or by any means, electronic or mechanical, including photocopying, recording, or any other information storage and retreival system, without express permission of the publisher.

Library of Congress Cataloging-in-Publication Data is on file with the publisher.

ISBN 9781790711499

www.ProjectEnye.com

#OWN YOUR ENYE

FOR EDUCATION

by Guadalupe Olvera Montes Hirt

with Denise Soler Cox

foreword

When I first learned about Project Eñye, I was in the midst of planning and coordinating the Student Leadership Institute (SLI) as part of Dual Language Education of New Mexico's La Cosecha Conference. The SLI brings together linguistically and culturally diverse students to focus on issues of identity, leadership, and the development of an asset-based perspective relative to their diverse backgrounds. Indeed, this was fervent ground for the mission of Project Eñye, and they happily agreed to support the leadership institute with breakout sessions and the screening of the being eñye video.

As stated on their webpage, "Project Eñye has one single and simple purpose... to transform how we think and speak about culture, identity, and what it means to belong." Some of the students that attend our institute are confident and competent in the languages and cultures that surround them. Other students may value bilingualism, biliteracy, and biculturalism as assets, but the process of assimilation and the constant pressures of the language of power have left many others with feelings of self-loathing and shame. In short, many of us reach a point where we become painfully aware that our own elders, our own people, view us as deficient in the language and culture of our parents and grandparents. Suddenly, we are not considered to be sufficiently or legitimately connected to the cultural and linguistic legacies to which we were born. At the same time, we may even find that our own country perceives us to be equally insufficient in our ability to embrace the mainstream society and cultural nuances dictated by the English language and the dominant culture. What a conundrum!

foreword

Until now, when has this reality ever been deliberately and caringly addressed within our homes and our classrooms? In my personal journey, I can recall many a time when I felt deficient and defective when it came to my emerging bilingual self that was linguistically and culturally different in ways that were more complex than the label may imply. It is this sense of deficiency and defectiveness that Project Eñye courageously addresses through a multitude of activities that can easily be integrated in any humanities curriculum and other content areas as well. One of the activities in the book that struck a chord with me as a former educator, parent, and forever eñye was the module entitled, My Family's Native Language. This activity supported participants to recognize the practical skills and intrinsic benefits of being bilingual, establish an initial profile based on self-perceptions related to the heritage language, and identify clear goals on the journey towards self-acceptance and language recovery. What a quick, succinct, and beautiful activity to nurture our linguistically and culturally different students!

Project Eñye Co-Founders Guadalupe Olvera Montes Hirt and Denise Soler Cox must be commended for creating the #OwnYourEñye Education Workbook. We've needed this hug for a long time! Thank you both for taking the leadership and the first steps, both personally and professionally, towards healing a hurt that manifests itself over multiple generations! Son ejes de la cultura y la humanidad.

Adrian is first and foremost a father of two children. In the professional setting, he is a senior associate with the Center for the Education and Study of Diverse Populations (CESDP) at New Mexico Highlands University and a former coordinator for professional learning at Dual Language Education of New Mexico (DLeNM). He has over 27 years as an educator in collaboration and support of culturally and linguistically different students.

prologue

INTRODUCTION AND REFLECTION

Welcome to the Eñye student experience! This workbook was designed to help the sons and daughters of immigrant parents recognize, reconcile, and embrace the duality of being a multicultural American.

We are excited for you to go on this journey and begin to understand who you are at the very core of your being. You will be asked to be authentic, vulnerable, but most importantly, brave. Know that these activities and discussions may be tough because they will challenge you to think and talk about topics that we typically don't talk about with others, even our own families. You will stir up emotions and feelings that may make you feel uncomfortable at times, but please know that you are not alone.

If you are willing to authentically share your story, you will unlock the power, resilience, and virtue to overcome what has held many of us back – the feeling that we never felt "enough" to seasmlessly fit into our American life or our parent's country of origin.

We hope the experiences and conversations in this workbook open your eyes, hearts, and minds to the beauty that comes with being unapologetically you. We also hope to help you learn to value the importance of being different. May your difference spark a curiosity to become culturally aware and respectful so we can all feel like we belong.

Abrazos,

Guadalupe Olvera Montes Hirt   Denise Soler Cox

PROJECT EÑYE
creed

Life is too short not to know where you belong.

Look to the Eñye inside to guide you home.
You are not alone, even if you feel like it.
Reject shame. Accept yourself. Trust your gut.
Who you are IS good enough.
Celebrate what makes you, YOU.
Own Your Eñye story and share it.
My story matters. Your story matters.
Vulnerability is not a sign of weakness;
it is a gateway to strength.
Boldly walk the line between birthright
and heritage with unwavering pride.
We are 100% American.
We are 100% Eñye.
Share this experience with the world,
and see what happens.
An Eñye's cultural awakening
can change everything.

table OF CONTENTS

INTRODUCTION AND REFLECTION:	4
KEEPING YOUR VOICE AUTHENTIC:	6
FOR THE LOVE OF FOOD:	16
MY RELATIONSHIP WITH LANGUAGE	26
BEYOND THE REFLECTION IN THE MIRROR:	36
CULTURAL IDENTITY THROUGH ART:	46
UNAPOLOGETICALLY ME:	58
PRESERVING MY CULTURE:	72

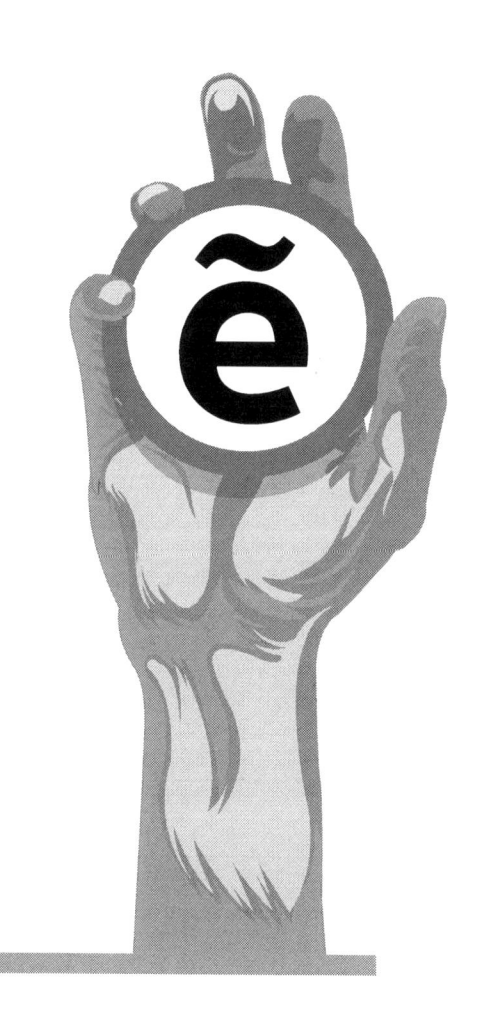

© 2019 Project Eñye – All rights reserved. No part of this publication may be reproduced or transmitted in any form or by any means, electronic, mechanical, including photocopying, recording, or any other information storage and retrieval system, without express permission of the publisher.

INTRODUCTION AND REFLECTION
overview

MODULE 1: WHAT "BEING EÑYE" MEANS TO ME?

As you saw in the film, Eñyes often feel caught between two worlds. Many Eñyes have expressed not feeling "American-enough" at school or with friends and also not feeling "Latino-enough" around native speakers or extended family — yet they are enough! In the film, you saw how this dual-state of identity consciously and subconsciously manifested in different ways and shaped how the characters saw themselves and how the world saw them.

💡 Have you ever felt caught between two worlds?

TIME TO BE AUTHENTIC

:: Write one word that best describes the film. Explain why you selected this word.

_____

:: Describe how you felt after watching the film. Write down three emotions/feelings you experienced. Did a particular part of the movie trigger a stronger emotion than you were expecting? If yes, how?

_____
_____
_____
_____
_____
_____

:: In the film, Denise often says she didn't feel "Latina-enough." What do you think that means? Have you ever felt not "[fill in your ethnicity/nationality]-enough?" Explain.

_____
_____
_____
_____
_____
_____

PROJECT EÑYE **STUDENT WORKBOOK**

INTRODUCTION AND REFLECTION
overview

MODULE 1: WHAT "BEING EÑYE" MEANS TO ME?

:: Identify one scene from the film that impacted you the most. Explain. How did it impact you?

_____
_____
_____
_____
_____
_____
_____
_____
_____

:: How did the film make you feel overall?

_____
_____
_____
_____
_____
_____
_____

:: Did the film remind you of anything you've experienced? Explain.

_____
_____
_____
_____
_____
_____
_____
_____
_____

KEEPING YOUR VOICE AUTHENTIC
overview

MODULE 1: THE ART OF IDENTITY CODE-SWITCHING

Keeping your voice authentic is the practice of maintaining a conscious balance between the American environment we are immersed in daily and the [fill in your ethnicity/nationality] predispositions that are part of our family's heritage. We all have immigrant roots. The only difference is when our families immigrated to the United States. Depending on when that journey took place and how culture was passed down, many Eñyes and even 2nd, 4th, or even 7th generations find it difficult to keep their voice authentic.

As Eñyes, we effortlessly code-switch between these two states of existing "turning on" or "turning off" our cultural tendencies or modifying our pronunciation, mannerisms, or cultural practices to better fit in with the dominant culture. In the film, Denise talks about her mom changing her name from **"Lolin to Dolores"** when they moved to Westchester.

💡 Recall a time when you code-switched between your "American" side and your "[fill in your ethnicity/nationality]" side. How did that make you feel?

TIME TO LEARN ABOUT YOUR CLASSMATES

Pair up with a classmate and answer/discuss the following questions together.

:: Have you ever been made to feel you were acting "too white" or "not [fill in your ethnicity/nationality]-enough" by family or friends? Explain.

PROJECT EÑYE **STUDENT WORKBOOK**

KEEPING YOUR VOICE AUTHENTIC
overview

MODULE 1: THE ART OF IDENTITY CODE-SWITCHING

:: Have you experienced prejudicial remarks or behavior because of your identity? Explain what happened, and how did you react? How did it make you feel?

_____
_____
_____
_____
_____

:: Have you ever criticized others because they didn't "measure up" to your standards of what a particular ethnic group/nationality should act like? Why do you think you acted that way?

_____
_____
_____
_____
_____

:: Do you feel like you can be your whole self at school, or do you have to suppress one side of you to fit in? Why do you feel that way?

_____
_____
_____
_____
_____

KEEPING YOUR VOICE AUTHENTIC
overview

MODULE 2: FEELING CAUGHT BETWEEN TWO WORLDS

Belonging is a basic human need just like food and water. No one is exempt from it, and it is an experience we desire at every stage of our life. In the film, "being eñye," Denise talks about not feeling Latina-enough because she was light-skinned, didn't speak Spanish well, and didn't know her culture as well as she thought she should. On the flip side, she also didn't feel American-enough because she was immersed in Puerto Rican culture at home, ate Puerto Rican foods, and didn't look like the other students in her school.

💡 Are there things about yourself that make you feel like you don't belong?

DIRECTIONS

Interview an adult in your life (teacher, family member, mentor, etc.), and ask if at some point they felt that they didn't belong because of their ethnicity, gender, or religion. See next page for sample interview questions to ask them.

DELIVERABLES

Write a diary entry about the interviewee's experience in the first person from their perspective. However, instead of ending it with the interviewee not feeling like they belong, how would you re-write the ending for them? What would you have them do instead? Be sure to decorate the journal entry for visual appeal.

KEEPING YOUR VOICE AUTHENTIC
overview

MODULE 2: FEELING CAUGHT BETWEEN TWO WORLDS

SAMPLE QUESTIONS

1. Where were your parents born? Where were you born?

2. What is your ethnicity/nationality?

3. Recall an occasion when you felt not American-enough or [fill in your ethnicity/nationality]-enough. Describe what happened.

4. How did that make you feel?

5. How did you handle the experience?

6. Have you ever shared this story with someone before? Why or why not?

KEEPING YOUR VOICE AUTHENTIC
overview

MODULE 3: STEREOTYPES

You are an individual. Don't be so quick to judge based on what people look like. In the film, Denise talks about being called a "spic" in middle school because she was the only Latina in the school. Other characters like Flaco Navaja talk about **"going from one extreme to the other,"** and at one point being labeled a **"black militant"** as he struggled with his own identity.

According to Dictionary.com, a stereotype is a "widely held but fixed and oversimplified image or idea of a particular type of person or thing."

💡 Why do you think people stereotype others?

DIRECTIONS

Review the following statements. Write a rebuttal statement to refute these stereotypes.

:: Multicultural people are uneducated and poor.

_____
_____

:: Asians are cold and emotionless.

_____
_____

:: People who don't speak English are undocumented immigrants.

_____
_____

PROJECT EÑYE **STUDENT WORKBOOK**

KEEPING YOUR VOICE AUTHENTIC
overview

MODULE 3: STEREOTYPES

:: Black women are bossy and over-bearing.

_____
_____

:: Women are not equal to their male counterparts.

_____
_____

:: Latinos/as/xs, Native Americans, and African Americans don't work hard enough, and that's why they don't move up in the corporate world.

_____
_____

TIME TO BE AUTHENTIC

:: Have you ever been stereotyped? Explain what happened, and how you handled it. If you heard friends or family stereotyping someone else, what would you do?

_____
_____
_____
_____

:: Describe a time when you found yourself stereotyping someone else? Why do you think you did that? How do you think it made that person feel? What can you do today to make sure this stereotype is not perpetuated?

_____
_____
_____
_____

KEEPING YOUR VOICE AUTHENTIC
overview

MODULE 4: THEN AND NOW

Speaking up or self-advocating can be scary and requires courage, but it can also be very empowering. In the film, Denise talks about her family's name being pronounced **"soh-ler versus soh-lair"** when they moved to Westchester, a predominantly Anglo community. Why do you think we change things about ourselves, allow others to change things about us, or pronounce words/names differently?

Life requires compromises, but not at the expense of your self-worth. In these situations, speaking up and not compromising requires confidence, courage, and a willingness to feel uncomfortable. Many people avoid confrontation because they believe it will be a negative experience; however, when done with grace and mutual respect, self-advocacy can be very empowering.

💡 Think of a time when you didn't speak up or self-advocate. Were you happy with the outcome?

DIRECTIONS

Take a few minutes to recall instances in the past when you either changed or allowed others to influence something about yourself. Describe the scenario in the first column, and then re-write how you would handle that situation now.

KEEPING YOUR VOICE AUTHENTIC
overview

MODULE 4: THEN AND NOW

THEN	NOW

MY CULTURAL PLEDGE

:: Write a promise below that you can work towards to be more culturally respectful and lead by example. For instance, I pledge to pronounce a person's name as correctly as possible. If I don't know how to pronounce it, I will ask them for help.

I pledge to _____

_____

_____

_____

Name _____ Date _____

Signature _____

KEEPING YOUR VOICE AUTHENTIC
overview

MODULE 5: CUMULATIVE PROJECT

There is great value in being both American and [fill in your ethnicity/nationality]. Our society is multicultural and in order for our society to evolve and thrive, it is important that we all do our part to have an open mind and learn and respect other cultures. There is inherent value in being different, but before that value can truly be appreciated, you need to recognize that being different is not a bad thing or a threat; it is simply unfamiliar and requires further learning.

💡 When is the last time you took a moment to learn about another ethnicity/nationality?

DIRECTIONS

Create a poster collage, drawing, or multimedia presentation with things that represent the value/beauty of your bicultural or multicultural background.

BRAINSTORMING QUESTIONS

:: I am [fill in your ethnicity/nationality].

_____

:: Why is being [fill in your ethnicity/nationality] beautiful?

_____
_____
_____

KEEPING YOUR VOICE AUTHENTIC
overview

MODULE 5: CUMULATIVE PROJECT

:: Is it important to support and respect diversity and different cultures? Why?

_____

_____

:: Share one thing you can actively do to support a multicultural society?

_____

_____

BRAINSTORMING GRID

Use the grid below to help you think of ways you are proud to be [fill in your ethnicity/nationality].

VALUES	FOODS	LANGUAGE
RELIGION	MUSIC	HOLIDAYS/TRADITIONS

FOR THE LOVE OF FOOD
overview

MODULE 1: GATHERING TOGETHER AT THE TABLE

Coming together and sharing a meal is one of the most communal and universal human acts a person can be a part of in almost every corner of the world. Food creates an opportunity to provide nourishment and also share who you are with others. It is a beautiful way to celebrate, pass down, and learn about other cultures — after all, we all have to eat!

For Eñyes, food is a tangible way to connect to their parent's country of origin and embrace their Latino/a/x side. Whether it's learning a family recipe, helping prepare a meal, food shopping with parents, or simply eating, food does not discriminate or cast judgments. Instead, it invites everyone to the table.

💡 If you could invite three people to join you at the table to enjoy a cultural dish, who would you invite?

WHAT'S ON YOUR PLATE?

While foods or ingredients may be different from one culture to the next, nearly every culture has "common foods" that accompany every dish or are frequently made. Complete the grid on the following page individually and then pair up with a classmate to compare and contrast your answers.

FOR THE LOVE OF FOOD
overview

MODULE 1: GATHERING TOGETHER AT THE TABLE

:: What is your ethnicity/nationality?

AT MY TABLE	AMERICAN EQUIVALENTS
SIDE DISHES	**SIDE DISHES**
MAIN ENTRÉE	**MAIN ENTRÉE**
BEVERAGES	**BEVERAGES**
DESSERTS	**DESSERTS**

© 2019 Project Eñye – All rights reserved. No part of this publication may be reproduced or transmitted in any form or by any means, electronic, mechanical, including photocopying, recording, or any other information storage and retrieval system, without express permission of the publisher.

#OWN YOUR EÑYE

FOR THE LOVE OF FOOD
overview

MODULE 2: CULTIVATING AN APPETITE FOR CULTURE

Food is a delicious and fun way to learn about other cultures one dish at a time. Food can also be a great way to learn even more about one's own culture, since foods can sometimes vary by geography or accessability to ingredients. Food has many symbolic meanings, and nearly every culture has its own foods and table etiquette. Since everyone enjoys eating, heritage foods are a beautiful way to preserve and share culture with others.

> Recall a time when you were at a friend's house and you sampled one of their cultural dishes. What did you eat?

DIRECTIONS

Pick a food from the "Gathering together at the table" exercise on the previous page and create a recipe sheet.

FOR THE LOVE OF FOOD
overview

MODULE 2: CULTIVATING AN APPETITE FOR CULTURE

DELIVERABLES

The 8x11 recipe sheet must include the following components:

- Ethnicity/nationality label (i.e. Mexican, Lebanese, Indian, etc.)
- Category (side dish, entrée, dessert, beverage)
- Name of recipe and whose recipe it is
- List of ingredients
- Preparation instructions
- Table etiquette for eating this dish (i.e. eat it with your hands, eat it from a community bowl, etc.)
- Drawing or photograph of dish
- Descriptive paragraph
    - Why did you pick this dish?
    - When is this dish served at your house?
    - Who makes the dish at your house?
    - How often do you eat this dish?
    - Anything else you want to share about the dish?

FOR THE LOVE OF FOOD
overview

MODULE 3: SPECIAL OCCASIONS AND HOLIDAYS

Food and family are intrinsically connected. Whether it's everyday meals, special celebrations, or the holidays, food is a fantastic way to share nourishment and spend time with loved ones. In the movie "being eñye," Denise shares that her house smelled like a Puerto Rican house. **"It smelled like sofrito and platanos frying on a pan."** Coming home to the smells in the kitchen of your childhood home is often a fond memory for many.

💡 Recall your childhood kitchen. What aromas do you remember smelling?

Food is a strong ethnic connector and plays a big part in many cultures, regardless if we eat arroz con pollo, dal mahkni, dim sum, kisra, or moussaka. Our memories are strongly tied to smells, and for many, these smells often elicit strong emotions and vivid memories of time spent with loved ones. Many Eñyes have a nostalgic bond with their parent's country of origin, a place they feel connected to but will never truly be a part of because they were born in America. Food is one way Eñyes stay connected to their familial roots that doesn't require a passport.

TIME TO EAT

The holidays are usually designated times when family and extended family gather around the table to share a meal. Read the blog entry that Denise wrote about making pasteles de yuca for Christmas in the appendix. What dishes are prepared in your home during the holidays?

FOR THE LOVE OF FOOD
overview

MODULE 3: SPECIAL OCCASIONS AND HOLIDAYS

DIRECTIONS

Pick a holiday that your family celebrates and draw a plate with the various food items that you would expect to see on your plate.

DELIVERABLES

Draw a plate topped with your family's special holiday foods. For your project:

- Draw each food item and label it accordingly
- List what family member prepares each food item
- Share why you enjoy the foods on your plate

FOR THE LOVE OF FOOD
overview

MODULE 4: FOOD SHAME

As children, we typically grow up eating cultural foods at home and are usually not exposed to the dominant food culture until school. During those formative years, we eat what we are served and don't really think much about the differences between "our food" and "their food." It isn't until school when we become more aware of these differences and can sometimes feel out of place because of our cultural foods.

Both Lupe and Denise remember feeling out of place at the lunch table for eating cultural foods that weren't like the "normal" foods their friends had in their lunches. To try and fit in, both asked their moms for PB&J sandwiches instead of the traditional burritos and platanos maduros their moms packed in their lunch boxes. How do you think their moms reacted?

💡 Have you ever asked your parents for something different?

TIME TO REFLECT

Answer these questions and then be prepared to participate in a group discussion.

:: Think of a time when you felt embarrassed or uncomfortable by the foods your parents packed in your lunch. What food embarassed you? What happened? How did you feel?

_____
_____
_____
_____
_____
_____
_____

PROJECT EÑYE **STUDENT WORKBOOK**

FOR THE LOVE OF FOOD
overview

MODULE 4: FOOD SHAME

:: Recall a time when someone brought something different in their lunch. How did you react? With curiosity or criticism? Explain.

___

:: Lupe and Denise wanted PB&J sandwiches instead of their mothers' home-made lunches. What foods did you want to trade your food for and why? What happened?

___

FOR THE LOVE OF FOOD
overview

MODULE 5: CUMULATIVE PROJECT

Food is a great and simple way to appreciate, understand, and share culture with others. Everyone can appreciate great food, regardless of what ethnic group inspires the dish. By being open to tasting other dishes and trying something new, you can gain a better understanding of the flavors, ingredients, and traditions that make other cultures as special and unique as your own. In some instances, we combine foods to create our own dining experience. Lupe remembers her mom serving arroz (rice) with pizza, and Denise remembers eating maduros (deep fried sweet plantains) with scrambled eggs.

💡 What cultural foods do you like to combine?

DIRECTIONS

Pick a dish from a different culture that you enjoy eating and do some research to learn more about the dish. Use the questions on the following page to guide your research.

DELIVERABLES

Create a PowerPoint presentation about your selected dish to present to the class. Presentation must include:

- Name of dish
- Country of origin
- Overview of the dish and why you picked it
- Pictures or drawings of the dish

FOR THE LOVE OF FOOD
overview

MODULE 5: CUMULATIVE PROJECT

RESEARCH QUESTIONS

:: When, where, and with whom did you first eat this dish?
_____
_____

:: Is this dish eaten every day or only on special occasions? If it is eaten on special occasions, does the dish have a special signficance?
_____
_____

:: In what way is it served or eaten?
_____
_____

:: How is the dish prepared?
_____
_____

:: What are the main ingredients?
_____
_____

:: Why did you pick this dish?
_____
_____

MY RELATIONSHIP WITH
language

MODULE 1: MAKING PEACE WITH THE PAST

As children, we are a product of what our parents choose to teach us. Sometimes, parents succumb to social pressures and make decisions to "fit in" with the dominant culture. There is tremendous social pressure around language and often immigrant parents are faced with the decision to pass down their native language or adopt the dominant language. Unfortunately, many parents decide not to teach their children their native language. Parents hope this decision will protect their children and make their transition in the U.S. easier.

💡 If you were in your parent's shoes, what would you do? Why?

As Eñyes or American-born children to immigrant parents, we are the generation that determines, for the most part, how our culture evolves in the U.S. While you can't go back and change the past, you can choose to make peace with it and take steps, big or small, to change your future. The beauty of life is it's never too late for a fresh start.

TIME TO REFLECT

Answer these questions on your own and be prepared to share in a group discussion.

:: **What language did you speak first?**

_____

:: **Did everyone in your family speak the same language or were other languages spoken in the home? If there were other languages spoken, what were they and who spoke them?**

_____

_____

PROJECT EÑYE STUDENT WORKBOOK

MY RELATIONSHIP WITH
language

MODULE 1: MAKING PEACE WITH THE PAST

Rate your comfort level speaking your parent's primary language in the following settings using the scale below.

1 – Not comfortable >>> 10 – Very comfortable

	At home with family.
	At your friend's house.
	When visiting extended family living in your parent's country of origin.
	With friends in public spaces (i.e. mall, library, etc.).
	With family in public spaces (i.e. mall, library, etc.).
	In the classroom.

List three words that describe how you feel about knowing, or not knowing how to speak your parent's native language.

1. _____
2. _____
3. _____

:: **Reflecting upon your feelings around lanugage, what would you keep or change from this language experience?**

_____
_____
_____
_____

MY RELATIONSHIP WITH language

MODULE 2: IDIOMS AND SAYINGS IN OTHER LANGUAGES

"It's raining cats and dogs."

"I see the light."

"It's a piece of cake."

Just like in English, foreign languages have idioms, sayings and expressions that mean more than face value. Typically, heritage or native speakers have no problem understanding these peculiar and funny sayings because they're familiar with the culture; however, others may need a little help understanding them.

💡 Do you have a favorite idiom or saying you like to use?

DIRECTIONS

Interview family members to create a presentation that includes your top three favorite idioms, common phrases, sayings, or expressions in your parent's native language. Write or orally learn the saying in your parent's native language, translate it "literally" into English, and then describe the meaning behind it.

MY RELATIONSHIP WITH language

MODULE 2: IDIOMS AND SAYINGS IN OTHER LANGUAGES

DELIVERABLES

The presentation can be either visually or orally delivered, but must include the following components:

- Ethnicity/nationality label (i.e. Mexican, Lebanese, Indian, etc.)
- Expression presented in your family's native language
- Expression "literally" translated in English
- A 2-3 sentence explanation of what the expression means
- Pick one saying and phoenetically write it out to teach the class how to say it on presentation day

MY RELATIONSHIP WITH
language

MODULE 3: THE LANGUAGE POLICE

Language is a huge part of a culture, and it is often the single biggest source of guilt and shame for Eñyes. Friends, extended family, colleagues, strangers and even the media appoint themselves as the "language police" measuring your "enoughness" based on how well you speak the langague. These external sources can magnify our own guilt and shame making it extremely difficult for Eñyes to forgive, but most importantly, accept themselves as imperfectly-perfect cultural beings.

In the film "being eñye," there is a scene when Denise and Lupe are sitting on the couch talking about Lupe's shame and embarrassment around her limited ability to speak Spanish. The film then cuts to a scene where she's speaking Spanish on camera fluently, yet she still doesn't think it is good enough.

💡 Why do you think she feels that way? Can you relate?

REFLECTION TIME

:: Think of a time when you were made to feel less than by the "language police" because of your language abilities. What happened? How did you feel? Did you say anything? If you can't think of a time when you were called out, think of a time when you were embarrassed by your parent's inability to speak fluent English. What happened, and how did it make you feel?

_____
_____
_____
_____
_____
_____
_____

PROJECT EÑYE **STUDENT WORKBOOK**

MY RELATIONSHIP WITH
language

MODULE 3: THE LANGUAGE POLICE

_____

_____
_____
_____
_____
_____
_____

CLASSROOM PLEDGE

:: As a student in this class, I pledge to do my part to keep the "language police" out of our classroom. I will do this by:

_____
_____
_____
_____
_____
_____
_____

Name _____   Date _____

Signature _____

MY RELATIONSHIP WITH language

MODULE 4: MY ROLE IN PRESERVING MY FAMILY'S LANGUAGE

Children are a mix of their parent's heritage and the North American environment they live in. As such, some may fluently know their parent's native language; others may know a little, while others maybe were not taught the language at all. Language is a powerful way to celebrate a culture. As children living in the U.S., it is important we do our part to learn and preserve our family's native language, but not to live up to a "language police" standard, rather because you want to do it for your own personal development.

💡 What would it mean to you to know your family's heritage language? If you know how to speak the language, what value does that hold for you?

How important is it for you to keep this language alive?

☐ Very important

☐ Important

☐ Not important

Why? _____

List your three biggest barriers to being fluent.

1.

2.

3.

My language goal is to:

_____
_____

Start date _____   Goal date _____

PROJECT EÑYE STUDENT WORKBOOK

MY RELATIONSHIP WITH
language

MODULE 4: MY ROLE IN PRESERVING MY FAMILY'S LANGUAGE

If you want to work towards removing these barriers, below are a few ideas to help you reach this goal. Pick one from the list or come up with a new idea and commit to it.

- ☐ Ask your parents or family members to help you write sticky notes with the native language equivalent of items found in your house. Post them throughout your house and practice saying them daily.

- ☐ If you grew up speaking your family's native language, but don't feel you speak "well enough" or are out of practice, make a weekly commitment to schedule a call or meeting with a friend, teacher, or extended family member to practice speaking your family's native language with them.

- ☐ If you are working to learn the language, go to the library and check out a vocabulary book written in your family's native language or schedule a weekly sit down with a family member to learn/practice the language.

- ☐ Consider volunteering at a local non-profit that helps immigrants from your parent's country of origin to practice speaking the language.

- ☐ Other ideas?

_____

_____

_____

MY RELATIONSHIP WITH
language

MODULE 5: CUMULATIVE PROJECT

While English may be a global language, there are nearly 6,500 languages spoken around the world. Every language is an act of beauty beckoning your mouth to move a certain way to annunciate a syllable. In the end, one of the greatest gifts you receive from learning new languages is the ability to speak and connect with more people — after all the U.S. is only 1 of 195 countries in the world. While learning a different language requires willingness, commitment, and practice, it also calls for patience and grace to accept and be grateful for your abilities, no matter how minimal or advanced they may be.

💡 If you had a chance to learn a different language, what would you like to learn?

DIRECTIONS

Pick a city or town outside of the U.S. and write a travel blog highlighting key facts about the destination first-time visitors could use while visiting. Use the research questions on the following page as a guide.

DELIVERABLES

Write a 450-word travel blog. Blog must include:

- Name of selected city/town and at least one paragraph on the following:
    - Language
    - Food
    - Climate

- Include top activities to do or places to visit in this city/town

- A sidebar with five key phrases (i.e. where is the bathroom, please, nice to meet you, thank you) translated in this language a traveler could use while visiting

MY RELATIONSHIP WITH
language

MODULE 5: CUMULATIVE PROJECT

RESEARCH QUESTIONS

:: When was the language first created or used?

___

:: Is the language considered a "global" language or a "regional" language?

___

:: What are the top food staples in this region?

___

:: Is this city/town or region known for growing a certain type of food?

___

:: Describe the climate so people know what to pack.

___

:: When are the best times to visit and why?

___

:: Include fun or interesting facts you learned about this destination.

___

BEYOND THE REFLECTION IN THE
mirror

MODULE 1: MEDIA + ME

According to the Center for Media Literacy, "media literary is the ability to access, analyze, evaluate, and create media in a variety of forms." Today, there are many ways to consume media ranging from traditional TV, radio, advertising, newspapers, and magazines to emerging methods like text messages, memes, viral videos, social media, video games, and more. Regardless of the source, the common denominator is that all media is created by someone, and it is created for a particular reason. Understanding the reason is the basis of media literacy.

💡 How does the media affect how you see the world?

Given the sheer volume of media available, we often accept this content at face value and fail to "reality check" its source, facts, and message. This blind consumption can influence our perceptions and positively or negatively shape how we see and interact with others. For example, Latinos/as/xs are often times depicted as gang members, drug dealers, or thieves. In the film, Denise's friend Augie talks about how he **"stuck out like a sore thumb"** when he visited them in Westchester because of his dark skin. **"There was like a mystique about me and people were kind of even afraid of me before they even got to know me."**

CRITICAL THINKING

List the top three ways you consume media.

1. _____
2. _____
3. _____

PROJECT EÑYE **STUDENT WORKBOOK**

BEYOND THE REFLECTION IN THE
mirror

MODULE 1: MEDIA + ME

On a scale of 1-10, how often do you see your ethnic group represented in the media with 1 being never and 10 being always?

1   2   3   4   5   6   7   8   9   10

List the content platform and describe the way your ethnic group is depicted. Use your best judgment to determine if the depiction is positive, neutral, or negative.

PLATFORM	MEDIA DEPICTION	POSITIVE ( ) NEUTRAL ( ) NEGATIVE ( )
		POSITIVE ( ) NEUTRAL ( ) NEGATIVE ( )
		POSITIVE ( ) NEUTRAL ( ) NEGATIVE ( )
		POSITIVE ( ) NEUTRAL ( ) NEGATIVE ( )

Using the content platforms listed in the first question, pick an ethnic group that is different than yours. Describe how the media depicts that group and determine if the depiction is positive, neutral, or negative.

Ethnic group _____

PLATFORM	MEDIA DEPICTION	POSITIVE ( ) NEUTRAL ( ) NEGATIVE ( )
		POSITIVE ( ) NEUTRAL ( ) NEGATIVE ( )
		POSITIVE ( ) NEUTRAL ( ) NEGATIVE ( )
		POSITIVE ( ) NEUTRAL ( ) NEGATIVE ( )

Analyze your collective responses above. In your opinion, which media platforms are doing a better job than others depicting different groups and why?

_____

_____

What can you do to influence change in the media?

_____

_____

BEYOND THE REFLECTION IN THE
mirror

MODULE 2: MY CODE OF ETHICS

Our code of ethics usually comprises a combination of familial, cultural, and societal norms, standards, and beliefs. We learn the basics at home, either from our parents or extended family members. We use this framework as a guide to create our own code of ethics and help us become the person "I want to be when I grow up." Keep in mind that you have complete control over this framework and you can choose to change it at any time and any age. Your goal should be to create a code of ethics that makes you proud of the person you see in the mirror every day.

💡 Are you proud of who you see in the mirror?

DIRECTIONS

We pick clothes to wear for a variety of reasons, but it's all about how the clothes makes us feel. Using the family t-shirt template on the following page, decorate one t-shirt with items, symbols, or words that represent your family, and then decorate the second t-shirt with items that represent you.

DELIVERABLES

- T-shirt templates
- Compare and contrast the similarities and differences between both t-shirts

PROJECT EÑYE **STUDENT WORKBOOK**

BEYOND THE REFLECTION IN THE
mirror

MODULE 2: MY CODE OF ETHICS

FAMILY T-SHIRT
Explain the symbols, words, and items you selected to decorate the t-shirt.

_____
_____
_____
_____
_____
_____
_____

MY T-SHIRT
Explain the symbols, words, and items you selected to decorate the t-shirt.

_____
_____
_____
_____
_____
_____
_____

COMPARE AND CONTRAST
Look at both t-shirts and determine what is similar and what is different. Are you surprised? Why?

Similarities

_____
_____
_____

Differences

_____
_____
_____

BEYOND THE REFLECTION IN THE
mirror

MODULE 3: THE RACE TO BE ATTRACTIVE

While media and the dominant culture typically shape and set societal standards of attractiveness, there are also standards set within our own ethnicities/nationalities. These cultural standards can influence the way we feel and think about our physical appearance and can sometimes impact us more than societal beauty standards.

Issues around ethnic and racial identity are especially complex for Eñyes. Our heritage can be White, Native American, African, Mestizo, Asian or a combination of several; thus, creating varying shades of skin tones, eye color, hair texture, body frame, etc. In the film, there is a scene in the courtyard where Denise's brother and friends talk about how they thought Denise had it easier in school because of her complexion. **"I thought you had a free pass because, first of all, you're a light skinned Latina, you're pretty and you got guys around you that want to protect you."**

💡 How do you feel when others judge you based on societal or cultural standards of attractiveness?

WORD ON THE STREET

Fill in the following according to what you think your culture believes is physically attractive.

Eye color (specify color, big or small) _____

Hair type (curly, straight, long, short) _____

Hair color (blonde, brunette, redhead) _____

Body frame (slender, curvy, tall, short) _____

Skin color (light, medium, dark) _____

Other physical attributes you'd like to note? _____

PROJECT EÑYE **STUDENT WORKBOOK**

BEYOND THE REFLECTION IN THE
mirror

MODULE 3: THE RACE TO BE ATTRACTIVE

:: How did you learn about this cultural standard of attractiveness?

_____
_____
_____
_____

:: Do you fit this description? Regardless of your response, how does that make you feel?

_____
_____
_____
_____

:: Do people in your family fit this description? If yes, describe your relationship with them? How do you feel about them?

_____
_____
_____
_____

:: Do you agree with this description? If yes, why? If no, why not and what would you change about it?

_____
_____
_____
_____

BEYOND THE REFLECTION IN THE
mirror

MODULE 4: I AM PERFECTLY IMPERFECT

As human beings, we often get caught up in what others think. We alter ourselves to better fit in by changing our look, our interests, or our personality. While some may dismiss this as "an improvement" or "worth it to have friends" the reality is that it's not sustainable. Why? Because it's not you at the very core of your being. It's a modified version. Accepting yourself as a perfectly-imperfect person means that you are perfect in all aspects as long as you are YOU and don't try to be someone else. Our imperfections are what makes us special and one-of-a-kind.

For 17 years, Denise thought she was not "enough" to launch this Project and make this film. It was once she stopped caring what others thought and stopped believing the lie that she wasn't enough, that she found the courage to unapologetically own herself - imperfections and all.

💡 What perfect imperfection do you love the most about yourself?

DIRECTIONS

Affirmations are a wonderful way to recognize and own your amazingness and worth. These statements can be simple or descriptive, but they all must be positive. Write down four affirmations about your physical appearance and four affirmations about your character. Start your affirmatin with "I am."

Physical affirmations

1. _____
2. _____
3. _____
4. _____

PROJECT EÑYE STUDENT WORKBOOK

BEYOND THE REFLECTION IN THE
mirror

MODULE 4: I AM PERFECTLY IMPERFECT

Character affirmations

1. _____
2. _____
3. _____
4. _____

Pair up with someone else and complete the same assignment about your partner. Instead, start the sentence with "You are" because it's about them.

Physical affirmations

1. _____
2. _____
3. _____
4. _____

Character affirmations

1. _____
2. _____
3. _____
4. _____

BEYOND THE REFLECTION IN THE
mirror

MODULE 5: CUMULATIVE PROJECT

Change just doesn't happen on its own. We, as members of this society, need to be the change we want to see in our community and hopefully, in our world. Change can be big or small and take many forms, but in the end, change needs to advocate for positive improvement of something that negatively affects you or others. This entire Project was created because Denise was tired of feeling like she didn't belong. One day, she decided enough is enough and took a bold move to be a change agent and co-launch this Project and co-produce "being eñye." The outcome? Her commitment to being a change agent has helped thousands of Eñyes and Fr'eñyes be more culturally aware and accepting of themselves and others.

💡 What type of change could you put into motion?

DIRECTIONS

Select an issue/challenge that people of color face and design a program to address it. Remember, it can be big or small, but the goal is to create a wave of proactive and positive change in your classroom, school, community, or home.

BEYOND THE REFLECTION IN THE
mirror

MODULE 5: CUMULATIVE PROJECT

DELIVERABLES

Write an action plan that outlines how you will be a change agent. The plan should:

- Identify the problem you aim to help solve, and explain why it's important to address

- Outline your proposed solution and timeline to accomplish your plan

- If the plan requires purchasing items, be sure to include a budget and fundraising strategy

- Design a promotional poster showcasing your campaign

CULTURAL IDENTITY THROUGH
art

MODULE 1: IDENTITY POEM

Who am I? This is a simple question that people spend a lifetime trying to answer. For many of you, this Project may be the first time you talk about your identity, ancestral roots, or yourself as a cultural being with others. Eñyes can seamlessly go between their Latino/a/x and American worlds adapting as necessary to better fit in. What we may not realize is that this innate identity code-switching is an outward expression of our dual identity. This ability is the foundation that shapes our [fill in your ethnicity/nationality] American experience, allowing us to connect and make sense of these two different worlds.

Poetry is a powerful literary tool that people can use to express their emotions. Unlike other written formats, anyone can write poetry because it's not about MLA format or flowery vocabulary, but rather, it's about unfiltered expression. In the film, there is a scene where Sara Serrano, a New York-based Puerto Rican poet, performs her poem on camera. She talks about her dual identity, passions, and characteristics that make her...her.

💡 Have you ever read an identity poem that culturally resonates with you?

DIRECTIONS

Write an identity poem describing yourself. It can focus on one single thing about yourself or it can focus on your whole self. See appendix to read Sara's poem. The poem can follow a particular format like a Sonnet or Haiku or you can write a free verse poem and let the creativity just flow.

PROJECT EÑYE STUDENT WORKBOOK

CULTURAL IDENTITY THROUGH
art

MODULE 1: IDENTITY POEM

DIRECTIONS

Use the following reflection questions to help you write your poem.

- :: Physically and/or metaphorically describe who you see when you look in the mirror?
- :: What secrets do you safeguard that hold you back from revealing your true self?
- :: What emotions do you feel when you are immersed in your culture?
- :: What role do you think you play in your culture?
- :: What are you passionate about?
- :: Who do you want to be when you grow up?

CULTURAL IDENTITY THROUGH art

MODULE 2: ART, JUST LIKE BEAUTY, IS IN THE EYE OF THE BEHOLDER

Paintings have a beautiful way of bringing something to life. Perhaps it's an artist's use of colors, design, and style or maybe it's their technique or inspiration story that evokes an emotional connection. Have you ever come across a painting or photograph that just spoke to you? Art appreciation is a highly personal experience that not only allows you to connect to the painting, but also allows you to express your own sense of artistic style. The beauty of art is that it is truly in the eye of the beholder; there isn't a right or wrong way to make or appreciate art.

💡 Recall a time when you felt connected to a piece of artwork. How did it make you feel?

DIRECTIONS

Pick an art piece (photo, portrait, drawing, etc.) that you think best represents your culture, and then create your own version of this artwork. You can use another medium if you choose, but the final product must bear some resemblance to the original.

CULTURAL IDENTITY THROUGH
art

MODULE 2: ART, JUST LIKE BEAUTY, IS IN THE EYE OF THE BEHOLDER

DIRECTIONS

Pick an art piece (photo, portrait, drawing, etc.) that you think best represents your culture, and then create your own version of this artwork. You can use another medium if you choose, but the final product must bear some resemblance to the original.

CULTURAL IDENTITY THROUGH
art

MODULE 3: BOOKS AND CULTURE

DELIVERABLES

- A copy of the original image
- Your rendition of the original
- Written summary explaining why you picked this image and any modifications you made that are different from the original

Books have the power to prompt a series of reactions in readers. They can transport us to faraway lands, or even more powerful, offer us a story and cast of characters that mirror our reality and validate our cultural experiences. Throughout her travels with the film, Denise often praises authors like Sandra Cisneros, The House on Mango Street; Julia Alvarez, In the Time of the Butterflies; Esmeralda Santiago, When I was Puerto Rican; and Isabel Allende, The House of the Spirits for the profound effects their work had on her life and this Project.

While authors can't control how a book is interpreted, these authors bravely shared their lives in hopes of helping other Latino/a/x feel represented, and more importantly seen. Denise is often heard saying that these books saved her life and gave her hope.

💡 What book have you read that made you feel "seen?"

CULTURAL IDENTITY THROUGH
art

MODULE 3: BOOKS AND CULTURE

DIRECTIONS

Pick a [fill in your ethnicity/nationality] author that you are either familiar with or would like to learn more about. Write a 450-word biography on this author, and identify one of their book titles you pledge to read by the end of the school year. Use the questions below to guide your research.

:: What is the name of the author you selected, and why did you pick them?

:: Provide background information on this author. (Where are they from; when were they born; what ethnicity/nationality are they, etc?

:: How did you hear about this author? Did someone tell you about them? If yes, who? What was the context of the conversation?

:: Have you ever read books by this author? If yes, list books. What did you think of them? What is your favorite book by them?

CULTURAL IDENTITY THROUGH
art

MODULE 3: BOOKS AND CULTURE

READING PLEDGE

I pledge to read _____ (name of title)

by _____ (name of author) before _____ (date).

I promise to share this book with _____
_____ (name of person)

to expose others to the power of reading stories about our culture, traditions, families, and lives.

Name _____   Date _____

Signature _____

PROJECT EÑYE **STUDENT WORKBOOK**

CULTURAL IDENTITY THROUGH
art

MODULE 3: BOOKS AND CULTURE

:: What inspired them to start writing books?

_____
_____
_____
_____
_____

:: Have they won any awards or accolades for their books? If yes, list what books earned recognition.

_____
_____
_____
_____
_____

:: Do you think this author represents your culture well? Explain.

_____
_____
_____
_____
_____

CULTURAL IDENTITY THROUGH art

MODULE 4: MUSIC'S UNIVERSAL APPEAL

Music is one of the most beloved art forms that exist. It's used for many things like relaxation, prayer, meditation, teaching, or motivation. Unlike other art forms, music is universal and transcends language, ethnicity, age, gender, socio-economic status, and other labels that usually differentiate us. While its diverse range of sounds, styles, and instruments can evoke different emotions, music is one of the most iconic symbols of cultural identity.

In the film, Denise talks about how **"there was always old Puerto Rican music playing in the background"** at her house. While she didn't speak the language 100% or fully understand the lyrics, listening to her family's music helped her feel at home, even if beyond those four walls, Westchester felt like a strange place that was far from welcoming.

> Have you ever felt connected to something or somewhere because of music?

DIRECTIONS

As a younger child, you probably listened to whatever music your parents played on the radio. Perhaps there was a song for special occasions or get-togethers or maybe your parents sang you a special lullaby at nighttime. Pick a song that takes you back to a particular time and place when you felt "at home" and connected to your roots. Break into pairs and take turns answering the questions on the following page.

CULTURAL IDENTITY THROUGH
art

MODULE 4: MUSIC'S UNIVERSAL APPEAL

:: What's the title of the song that comes to mind when you think of home? Who's the artist?

_____
_____

:: Why does this song remind you of home?

_____
_____

:: What feelings do you get when you hear this song?

_____
_____

:: Did you hear this song for special occasions, or was it played all the time?

_____
_____

:: Who in your house liked to listen to this song?

_____
_____

:: Analyze the lyrics and summarize what the song is symbolically, not literally, trying to communicate.

_____
_____
_____

CULTURAL IDENTITY THROUGH
art

MODULE 5: CUMULATIVE PROJECT

Dance is a full body art form that uses the human body as an instrument of expression and communication. From the Cha Cha, Rancheras, Baile Folklorico, Cumbias, or Samba to Punjabi, Belly Dance, Reggae or Kizomba, our world is full of thousands of dance styles that are performed for myriad of reasons. While you can learn about a culture through Internet or book research, dance is a highly immersive method that you can use to educate others and educate yourself about the dance traditions that make each culture beautifully unique.

In the film, Lance Rios talks about how there are a lot of people that fault him for not knowing Spanish completely but he goes on to say that **"I can guarantee you that I can dance better salsa, merengue, bachata than them. I guarantee it."** That was how he connected to his culture, and he wasn't letting others take that away from him.

💡 Is there a cultural dance you enjoy seeing performed, or you enjoy dancing?

CULTURAL IDENTITY THROUGH art

MODULE 5: CUMULATIVE PROJECT

DIRECTIONS

Pick three cultural dance moves, and find videos of these dances being performed. Use the videos to design a video meme for each dance to present in class. Be sure to provide catchy copy that relates to the cultural dance. You will be asked to present two interesting/fun facts about each dance move, and play the video memes in class.

DELIVERABLES

- Pick three cultural dance moves and create a video meme for each one
- Oral presentation highlighting region/location the dance originated, name of it, and two interesting facts about each dance move
- Play each video meme in class

UNAPOLOGETICALLY me

MODULE 1: MENTAL RESET

As human beings, we must actively and consciously embrace diversity and stand up to discrimination. We must reset our mind and help others understand that being different is not bad, inferior, or valueless. It is the fundamental essence of our differences, both inside and outside of our families that make each one of us an irreplaceable, unique gift to this world. There is NO ONE else like you anywhere in this world.

This Project was founded to help you step into your amazingness, unleash your power, and wholeheartedly and unapologetically accept both sides of yourself. Just like the Eñye Creed states, we must **"Boldly walk the line between birthright and heritage with unwavering pride."**

What does "walk the line between birthright and heritage" mean to you?

REFLECTION TIME

Read the sentence below. What does this sentence mean to you? Break down your response using the following standpoints.

Each one of us is an irreplaceable, unique gift to this world. There is NO ONE else like you anywhere in this world.

:: From a cultural standpoint, this sentence means:

_____

_____

:: From an identity standpoint, this sentence means:

_____

_____

PROJECT EÑYE **STUDENT WORKBOOK**

UNAPOLOGETICALLY
me

MODULE 1: MENTAL RESET

:: From a familial standpoint, this sentence means:

_____

_____

:: From a youth standpoint, this sentence means:

_____

_____

FINDING COMMON GROUND

While many tend to focus on our differences, we have more in common than we think. For starters, we are all human beings, but perhaps there are other things in common that you never thought about.

Break out into small groups and write down what you all have in common and what only some of you have in common.

WHAT DO ALL OF US HAVE IN COMMON?	
1.	5.
2.	6.
3.	7.
4.	8.

WHAT DO SOME OF US HAVE IN COMMON?	WHO HAS THIS IN COMMON?
1.	
2.	
3.	
4.	

UNAPOLOGETICALLY
me

MODULE 2: BEING LESS GUARDED

Look around. You are probably surrounded by people who you see every day, but what do you really know about them? Odds are you probably know what they want you to know. As human beings, it is in our nature to be guarded, so we usually end up sharing a mere fraction of who we are with others. But what if, instead of being guarded, we allowed others to know more about us?

💡 When was the last time you let your guard down?

DIRECTIONS

Pair up with someone you usually don't hang out with or don't know. Take turns answering the following questions. Write down your partner's answers in your book, and your partner will do the same. Take your partner's answers and write a keynote introductory speech introducing them at a conference, awards ceremony, or industry event.

DELIVERABLES

- A 250-word keynote introductory speech to present in class

UNAPOLOGETICALLY me

MODULE 2: BEING LESS GUARDED

GETTING TO KNOW YOU

These are sample questions to guide the discussion.

What is your full name (including your middle name)?

_____

How old are you? _____ Siblings? _____

What ethnicity/nationality are you? _____

Are you an ☐ Eñye or a ☐ Fr'eñye?

w

List top 5 things your partner likes and doesn't like.

Like ….	Don't like ….
1. _____	1. _____
2. _____	2. _____
3. _____	3. _____
4. _____	4. _____
5. _____	5. _____

What do you want to be when you grow up? _____

What do you think is your best quality? _____

What is your favorite hobby/past time? _____

What is your favorite subject in school? _____

Name two interesting facts about yourself.

1. _____
2. _____.

UNAPOLOGETICALLY me

MODULE 3: THE EÑYE EFFECT

The Eñye Effect is what happens when two worlds collide and you are caught in the middle. Many Eñyes and first-generation Americans born to immigrant parents can relate to this state of existing. In the Latino/a/x world, it's all about the "collective" or the family. The collective is valued above the individual. We are never told that we are part of a collective; it's more of an unwritten rule and expectation. Enter the "self-reliant," also known as the North American ideology. In this ideaology, independence and personal pursuits are valued above the group. What do these ideologies have in common? Absolutely nothing.

If you are like us, nobody sat you down and gave you a cultural rule book. You were just expected to figure it out, but that is where the challenge and opportunity exists for Eñyes and others that come from a collective group. The Eñye Effect is all about understanding and recognizing when these two ideologies are happening at home, school, work, or with friends. Once you tap into that awareness, you now have the power to combine and leverage both ideologies to your advantage. It's knowing when to be a team player or when to put yourself above the collective.

💡 What idealogy do you mainly operate from?

UNAPOLOGETICALLY me

MODULE 3: THE EÑYE EFFECT

DIRECTIONS

Read the following scenarios and write a response based on what you think the collective and self-reliant would expect you to do. In the last exercise, use both ideologies to write a hybrid response.

Scenario 1 — Martha is the oldest daughter in a family of four. Her parents are from Mexico and she lives in Los Angeles with her family. She has been accepted to two universities, but one is in Phoenix and the other is in Los Angeles. The school in Phoenix has additional coursework that could provide greater opportunities for Martha than the school in Los Angeles.

:: From a collective standpoint, what should Martha do?

_____
_____
_____

:: From a self-reliant standpoint, what should Martha do?

_____
_____
_____

:: Now combine both standpoints, what could Martha do?

_____
_____
_____

UNAPOLOGETICALLY me

MODULE 3: THE EÑYE EFFECT

Scenario 2 — Marco was part of a two-person team at school that completed an assignment that the teacher thought was amazing. While each worked on the project, Marco completed 70% of the work because his teammate got tired. The teacher has asked for one person from the group to present the project to the teacher committee in return for bonus points. Marco wants to take the opportunity, but the other teammate wants it as well.

:: From a **collective** standpoint, what is Marco supposed to do?

_____
_____
_____

:: From a **self-reliant** standpoint, what is Marco supposed to do?

_____
_____
_____

:: Now **combine** both **standpoints**, what could Marco do?

_____
_____
_____

UNAPOLOGETICALLY
me

MODULE 3: THE EÑYE EFFECT

Scenario 3 – Cynthia turns 15 in five months, and her Puerto Rican parents want her to have a quinceñera, but she doesn't want a party. She has a few Latina friends, but she currently lives in a predominantly Anglo community. She is the youngest and the only daughter in a family of five.

:: From a collective standpoint, what is Cynthia supposed to do?

_____
_____
_____

:: From a self-reliant standpoint, what is Cynthia supposed to do?

_____
_____
_____

:: Now combine both standpoints, what could Cynthia do?

_____
_____
_____

UNAPOLOGETICALLY me

MODULE 3: THE EÑYE EFFECT

Scenario 4 — Luis is a high school senior and a great golf player. He wants to join the golf team after school, but his parents need him to come home to care for his siblings, ages 6 and 8, so they can go to work. This is his last chance to make the team and show potential college scouts his skills.

:: From a collective standpoint, what is Luis supposed to do?

_____
_____
_____

:: From a self-reliant standpoint, what is Luis supposed to do?

_____
_____
_____

:: Now combine both standpoints, what could Luis do?

_____
_____
_____

PROJECT EÑYE **STUDENT WORKBOOK**

UNAPOLOGETICALLY
me

MODULE 3: THE EÑYE EFFECT

Think of a recent decision or scenario you found yourself in that forced you to take one side (collective or self-reliant) over the other. Use the questions below to think through the outcome. Knowing what you know about these ideologies, re-write the outcome.

:: **Scenario**

_____
_____
_____

:: **From a collective standpoint, what should you have done?**

_____
_____
_____

:: **From a self-reliant standpoint, what should you have done?**

_____
_____
_____

:: **Now combine both standpoints, what could you have done?**

_____
_____
_____

UNAPOLOGETICALLY
me

MODULE 4: DO YOU ACCEPT YOURSELF?

If someone asked you today, "Do you accept yourself?" what would you say? It's an interesting question that many would probably automatically answer "yes" without fully understanding the depth of the question. Accepting ourselves for what we or others like about ourselves is easy, but what about the rest of us? Could you accept what you or others don't like about you? Self-acceptance is not a default mental state or something you can auto-switch on or off depending on the day. It is a state of being that requires self-love, grace, patience, forgiveness, and a life-long commitment to being the best version of yourself.

In the film, you saw Denise, Lupe, and many characters struggle to accept what they didn't like about themselves. It seemed impossible to forgive themselves for not being Latina-enough, not knowing how to speak Spanish well enough, not looking American-enough, and not being enough in general. Many of these characters are still working on self-acceptance, and you can too. It's not an overnight fix or even a year-long fix; it is one step at a time. However, the journey and the destination, as you can see from the ripple effects this Project is having on the world, are worth it!

ONE STEP AT A TIME

On the following page, there are five ways you can begin to shed negative thoughts about yourself, and begin to self-accept and unapologetically live your life. Take time to reflect and individually write down your responses.

UNAPOLOGETICALLY
me

MODULE 4: DO YOU ACCEPT YOURSELF?

---

1. **Set an intention to guide your daily thoughts.**
   Repeat your intention every day. By reminding yourself of your intention, you stay focused and will soon see the positivity you can attract and how this intention will subtly guide your actions.

   _____
   _____

2. **Write down one strength/achievement daily.**
   You are doing amazing things, both big and small, every single day. Keep a running list and you'll see how awesome you really are!

   _____
   _____

3. **Call out people that bring you down or simply walk away.**
   You will meet millions of people in your lifetime, but not all of them will be special. Don't waste your time; spend more time with people that make you feel special.

   _____
   _____

4. **Write down something you forgive yourself for daily.**
   We all make mistakes. Instead of beating yourself up for it, write down something you can do to fix it or learn from it and move on.

   _____
   _____

5. **Perform charitable acts.**
   Giving of yourself to help others is truly amazing. Find something you are passionate about and donate time on a consistent basis. You'll soon realize the magnitude of your actions.

   _____
   _____

UNAPOLOGETICALLY me

MODULE 5: CUMULATIVE PROJECT

Life is full of choices. While some choices will have a bigger effect on us than others, we are a product of our collective decisions. Sometimes we make choices not because we want to, but rather because we want to fit in; we don't want to challenge the status quo, or we just want to be liked by others. While others, like friends, family, or politicians, can significantly influence our decisions, we have to remember that the only person who will have to live with these decisions is you.

Through the Project, we have met many successful adult Latinos/as/x who have made the right decisions to get to where they are in their jobs, family, and life. These same Latino/as/xs also admitted believing that they felt like they needed to suppress their Latinidad to fit in, move up, or simply survive. It was disheartening to see these amazing, accomplished adults feel culturally lost.

💡 What do you think culturally lost means? Have you ever felt culturally lost?

DIRECTIONS

If you could give your future self some advice, what would you tell yourself? Take into consideration everything that you've learned and write a 450-word letter to your future self. Use the questions on the following page to guide your thinking.

UNAPOLOGETICALLY me

MODULE 5: CUMULATIVE PROJECT

:: What kind of person do you want to be when you grow up?

:: What role do you want culture to play in your life?

:: How important is it to keep your culture alive? What would you want your future self to do about it?

:: List 1-2 cultural or identity goals you want your future self to achieve?

:: How do you want to interact with others that are a different ethnicity than you?

:: What can you do to advocate cultural empathy in your community?

PLANNING AHEAD

List three goals for personal growth you can start working on now. Outline below what your future self could do to crush these goals even more.

Present – Three areas of personal growth	Future – Crushing these goals
1.	1.
2.	2.
3.	3.

PRESERVING MY culture

MODULE 1: MY FAMILY'S NATIVE LANGUAGE

As discussed in My Relationship with Language module, there is a vast range of language proficiency among Eñyes or American-born [fill in your ethnicity/nationality]. Some parents taught us their native language, and others did not. While the proficiency range may be wide, we can commit to using and building on what we know to do our part to preserve, pass down, and share our family's native language with future generations.

In addition to preserving our native language, being bilingual or multilingual opens up endless possibilities and empowers you with a multitude of practical skills and intrinsic benefits that put you at a greater advantage than monolinguals. Let's rid our hearts and minds of whatever negative feelings we have harbored about our language abilities and enthusiastically embrace positive and goal-oriented commitments to preserve and practice our family's native language.

💡 Reflect on the past week, are there things you would have done differently

ADVANTAGES OF BEING BILINGUAL OR MULTILINGUAL

List below as many practical skills and intrinsic benefits possible for each category.

Practical skills	Intrinsic benefits

PRESERVING MY culture

MODULE 1: MY FAMILY'S NATIVE LANGUAGE

On a scale of 1 – 10, rate your native language abilities to understand your starting point and chart your plan to get you to your desired target point.

Current speaking abilities.

1.   2.   3.   4.   5.   6.   7.   8.   9.   10.
Needs some love   Rock star status

Desired speaking abilities by _____ (fill in your target date)?

1.   2.   3.   4.   5.   6.   7.   8.   9.   10.
Needs some love   Rock star status

Current comprehension abilities.

1.   2.   3.   4.   5.   6.   7.   8.   9.   10.
Needs some love   Rock star status

Desired comprehension abilities by _____ (fill in your target date)?

1.   2.   3.   4.   5.   6.   7.   8.   9.   10.
Needs some love   Rock star status

COMMITMENT TIME

Using the ratings above, complete the action statement on the following page to help you get started. Remember, set yourself up for success. Write down language targets and action steps that are feasible. Ask family or friends for additional ideas or strategies to accomplish your goal. Good luck!

PRESERVING MY culture

MODULE 1: MY FAMILY'S NATIVE LANGUAGE

LEARNING TARGET

:: I want to:

_____
_____
_____
_____

:: I can accomplish this target by:

_____
_____
_____
_____

:: If I need help keeping on track, I can:

_____
_____
_____
_____

:: I want to learn/improve upon this ability because:

_____
_____
_____
_____

PROJECT EÑYE **STUDENT WORKBOOK**

PRESERVING MY culture

MODULE 1: MY FAMILY'S NATIVE LANGUAGE

In the first column, list things that could get in the way of you accomplishing this goal. In the second column, list what you can do to address these concerns.

Potential obstacles	How to overcome the obstacles

I got this! I will complete this language goal by

_____

Name _____ Date _____

Signature _____

PRESERVING MY culture

MODULE 2: MY CULTURAL MEMORY BOX

Living in the United States, a place different than where your parents grew up, can make it challenging to hold onto one's heritage. Factors like everyday life, ethnic mix of friends, our community, and a lack of awareness about the importance of keeping our heritage alive, make it even more difficult. While there are some factors we cannot control, we do have control over our own efforts. That is the beautiful thing about tomorrow. If you didn't make it happen today, you always have another chance tomorrow.

💡 What could you do different from this day forward to practice your family's heritage/culture?

DIRECTIONS

Create a memory box and place five items inside that remind you about a cultural tradition, occasion or moment/celebration that your family passed onto you or that you were a part of at some point in your life. Pick 1 of these 5 traditions to pass onto your family when you grow up.

DELIVERABLES

- A decorated cultural memory box with the following inside:
    o Five cultural items
    o A handwritten note committing to pass down 1 of the 5 experiences onto your family

- Oral presentation about your box and the items inside

PRESERVING MY culture

MODULE 2: MY CULTURAL MEMORY BOX

_____

Preserving my culture promise (Sample copy)

When I was _____ (age), I was taught a cultural tradition by _____ (name). The cultural tradition was _____ (name of tradition) and it was practiced in my family because _____

_____

_____

I promise to pass on this tradition to my family one day or share it with my friends because _____

_____

_____

Name _____ Date _____

Signature _____

PRESERVING MY culture

MODULE 3: MY FAMILY'S CULTURAL FOODS

It may not come as a shock, but one of the most popular ways people celebrate, pass down, and preserve their culture is through food. As discussed in For the Love of Food module, food is the center of many familial experiences and fond memories. Whether it's the smell of your favorite dish, the chismes (gossip) and laughter coming from the kitchen, or the trips to the carniceria (butcher shop) with your family to pick up the specialty ingredients, food is a delicious and beautiful way to share culture and nourish the body.

💡 How does food connect you to your heritage or family?

ADVANTAGES OF KNOWING MY FAMILY'S CULTURAL FOODS

Besides a full stomach, there are many personal and familial benefits to learning our family's cultural foods. List below as many benefits as possible for each category.

Personal benefits	Familial benefits

PRESERVING MY culture

MODULE 3: MY FAMILY'S CULTURAL FOODS

REFLECTION TIME

Answer the following questions to understand what is your current family food knowledge in order to build upon that knowledge.

List your top three favorite family dishes.

1. _____

2. _____

3. _____

Do you have written recipes for each of these dishes? If you don't, list the person that could give you the recipe.

1. ☐ Yes ☐ No _____
2. ☐ Yes ☐ No _____
3. ☐ Yes ☐ No _____

PRESERVING MY culture

MODULE 3: MY FAMILY'S CULTURAL FOODS

Have you ever prepared or helped prepare any of these dishes? If you have not, list the person you could contact to help you make the dish.

1. ☐ Yes ☐ No _____

2. ☐ Yes ☐ No _____

3. ☐ Yes ☐ No _____

Do you know the origin story of these dishes? If you don't, list the person that could share the story with you.

1. ☐ Yes ☐ No _____

2. ☐ Yes ☐ No _____

3. ☐ Yes ☐ No _____

What else do you want to know about your family's cultural foods?

_____
_____
_____
_____

PRESERVING MY culture

MODULE 3: MY FAMILY'S CULTURAL FOODS

LEARNING TARGET

:: I want to:

_____
_____
_____
_____

:: I can accomplish this target by:

_____
_____
_____
_____

:: If I need help keeping on track, I can:

_____
_____
_____
_____

:: I want to learn/improve upon this ability because:

_____
_____
_____
_____

PRESERVING MY culture

MODULE 3: MY FAMILY'S CULTURAL FOODS

In the first column, list things that could get in the way of you accomplishing this goal. In the second column, list what you can do to address this concern.

Potential obstacles	How to overcome the obstacles

PRESERVING MY culture

MODULE 3: MY FAMILY'S CULTURAL FOODS

I got this! I will complete this language goal by

Name _____   Date _____

Signature _____

PRESERVING MY culture

MODULE 4: MY FAMILY'S STORIES

For centuries, people have used the simple art of storytelling to entertain, educate, or teach life lessons. Perhaps you grew up listening to stories before bedtime, at the kitchen table, or at family gatherings. What you may have not realized at the time was that you were actively participating in a long-standing, ancestral practice to preserve and pass down culture.

Some stories are a representation of culture and tradition that are typically passed down from generation to generation creating unity and reinforcing a cultural group's connection to the past, present, and future. This oral tradition can include ancestral stories, fairy tales, folktales, myths, and legends. Lupe remembers her mom using the folktale about La Llorona to keep her and her siblings in check when they were misbehaving or the fairy tale about El Ratón to get them to brush their teeth.

💡 What was your favorite story to listen to as a young child?

PRESERVING MY culture

MODULE 4: MY FAMILY'S STORIES

STORIES FROM THE HEART

:: Write the name of a story you remember listening to at home or from relatives.

_____
_____
_____

:: Write the name of the person that used to tell the story? Did they use any special voices, clothes, or other props to tell the story? Describe below.

_____
_____
_____

:: What was the story about? What was your favorite part?

_____
_____
_____

As you remember this story, write down what emotions you are feeling and explain each feeling.

Emotion	Explanation

PRESERVING MY culture

MODULE 4: MY FAMILY'S STORIES

LEARNING TARGET

:: I want to:

_____
_____
_____
_____

:: I can accomplish this target by:

_____
_____
_____
_____

:: If I need help keeping on track, I can:

_____
_____
_____
_____

:: I want to learn/improve upon this ability because:

_____
_____
_____
_____

PROJECT EÑYE **STUDENT WORKBOOK**

PRESERVING MY
culture

MODULE 4: MY FAMILY'S STORIES

In the first column, list things that could get in the way of you accomplishing this goal. In the second column, list what you can do to address these concerns.

Potential obstacles	How to overcome the obstacles

I got this! I will complete this language goal by

_____

Name _____   Date _____

Signature _____

PRESERVING MY culture

MODULE 5: CUMULATIVE PROJECT

As Eñyes or American-born [fill in your ethnicity/nationality], many of us are not fully versed in our family's cultural roots. Some of us may know the language, but don't know the history. Others may know how to cook family recipes, but don't know our culture's history and so forth. In the previous pages, you made several commitments to change this reality.

Take a minute and recognize the potential impact from these commitments. How will these decisions change you or change how the world sees you? How will these decisions help you achieve cultural balance? The outcome for amazingness is truly infinite. While the road may not always be easy, don't forget to forever be culturally proud, confident, and vocal. You are the change our world needs to safeguard and value multiculturalism in North America.

PRESERVING MY culture

MODULE 5: CUMULATIVE PROJECT

DIRECTIONS

Compile the commitments that you made in the previous pages and lessons learned about yourself and others throughout this program, and write a reflection story recounting your experience and potential for growth.

DELIVERABLES

- A 450-word story summarizing your experience throughout this program
- Oral presentation reading story in class

Dear student,

Thank you for being part of this self-discovery cultural journey with us. Our sincere wish for you is that you find inner peace, self-love, and appreciation for all human beings.

While we have come to the end of this book, your journey is just beginning.

For many, our film stirs up emotions and feelings that are often hard to express, and talk about with others. By authentically completing this program and daring to be vulnerable, you have taken a huge leap in a new direction that we hope will be filled with confidence, cultural pride, authenticity, and respect for self and others.

We started out focusing on corporate America thinking that was our only audience. As mentioned in previous chapters, we met some amazing, successful, and talented Latinos/as/xs, but what we found were that many of these Eñyes were struggling to bring their "whole self" to work because they felt they needed to conform to the ideal standard to excel or be taken seriously.

Many of these Eñyes are in the midst of what you just completed — so be amazingly proud of yourself! Why do we tell you this? It is our collective hope that by delving into this type of inner work at your age, you will have the confidence, skills, and savvy to change the trajectory of your life and our future corporate America. So when you get to that leadership position, you are mentally, emotionally, and culturally aware and prepared. May you live an amazing life!

With much love and gratitude,

Abrazos,

Guadalupe Olvera Montes Hirt		Denise Soler Cox

Made in the
USA
Lexington, KY